MW01626933

Favorite Tales, Food & FUNtivities™

Once Upon A Recipe™

by Goosie and Julie

Illustrated by Omar H. Davis

We have expressed that safety is a key issue when working with children in the kitchen, but we remind anyone using this book that there are potential hazards and adults must also be careful. Neither the authors nor the publisher can assume responsibility for any accident or mishap caused by using this book.

© 2000 Once Upon A Recipe, LLC

All rights reserved. No part of this book may be reproduced or utilized in any form or by any means, electronic or mechanical, including photocopying, recording, or by any information storage and retrieval system, without permission in writing from Once Upon A Recipe, LLC

ONCE UPON A RECIPE PRESS
1006 Chancellor Avenue
Maplewood, New Jersey 07040

Printed in the United States of America ISBN 0-9704113-0-8 Library of Congress Control No.: 00-092548

Once Upon A Recipe, FUNtivities, Goosie, Shelley, Break An Egg and YUM! are trademarks of Once Upon A Recipe, LLC

Dear Grown-ups,

Once upon a time, I started combining well-known stories with food and cooking and discovered that I had a great recipe for family fun, nutritious eating and learning. This idea was inspired by my six-year-old son Luke and his friends who not only love listening to stories, but also like watching their "mommies" in the kitchen and are always asking to participate.

I began by adding a humorous twist to a favorite tale such as The Three Little Pigs and created tasty recipes such as "Pig-Faced Pizzas" and "Berry Pink Lemonade" that relate to the story. I coined these activities "FUNtivities". Then, came our chief chef and storyteller, Goosie, a silly-looking kid-sized goose who embodies the whimsy, charm and child in all of us. It was a natural 'recipe' for fun.

I shared this 'recipe' with children and adults throughout the country at special events, cooking classes, classrooms and in parenting publications. Soon I discovered that Once Upon A Recipe has universal appeal with endless opportunities for sharing good times and recording memories. Who can forget seeing a child's face beam with pride as he or she presents a cookie they just decorated, while the frosting drips onto the floor (and maybe the dog!)?

So, as Goosie and I like to say, "Let's Get Crackin'!" It's time for you and your child to cook up some FUNtivities, share the learning and eat some yummy treats!

Break An Egg! (That means good luck and good health in Goose.)

Julie Edelman

Table of Contents

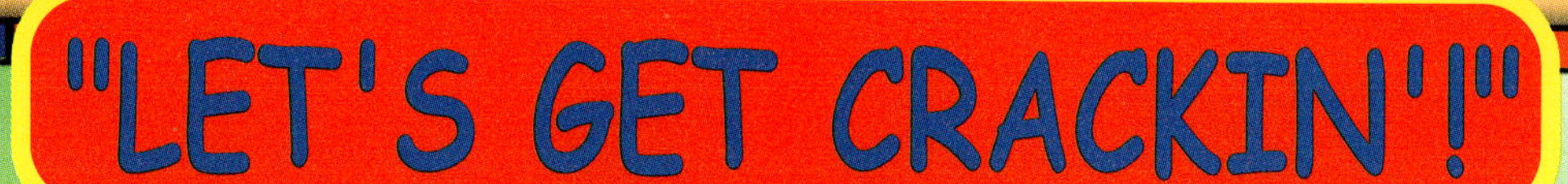

"LET'S GET CRACKIN'!"

TIPS & TOOLS

"HI, I'M GOOSIE™, Julie's friend, chief chef (say that three times fast!) and storyteller of Once Upon A Recipe. I'm here with our friend Shelley!

Heh! Heh! Heh!

He's an egg and our favorite yoke-ster. Every time he tells a joke he cracks himself up. Look for him throughout the boo

But now, let's get crackin'! Here are a few important safety tips and a list of helpful tools for grown-up helpers."

BE THERE! Grown-up supervision is required at all times. Never leave your child alone at any time in the kitchen especially near any hot stoves, ovens, knives, blenders or other electrical or dangerous appliances.

RELAX! Do not begin the Food FUNtivities when your child is hungry or you're in a hurry to make dinner or set your table. The foods are designed as snacks, not main meals. All the FUNtivities have been designed to encourage quality sharing time.

BE PREPARED! BE PATIENT! Review each recipe before involving your child. When cooking with children under three, cut and measure the ingredient before involving them. You'll be surprised how doin this will increase your patience!

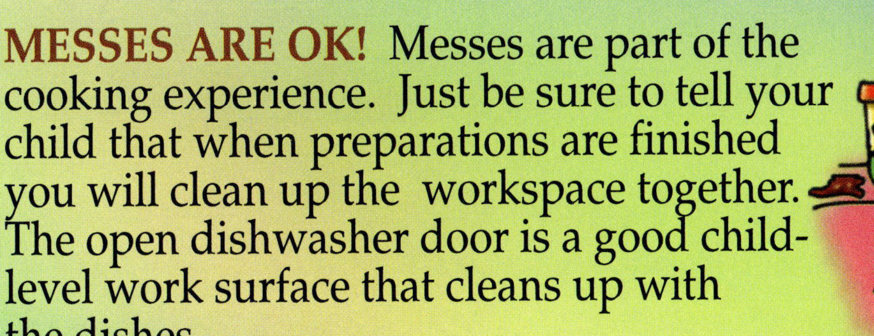

MESSES ARE OK! Messes are part of the cooking experience. Just be sure to tell your child that when preparations are finished you will clean up the workspace together. The open dishwasher door is a good child-level work surface that cleans up with the dishes.

GO WITH THE FLOW! Let your child substitute ingredients. If too much or too little of an ingredient is added, it won't hurt these recipes. The goal is to have children want to eat them as well as make them so they will be open to trying new and even healthier foods!

SHARE RULES AND GUIDELINES WITH YOUR CHILD.
Remind them to:

1. Always wash hands before cooking.
2. Wear an apron so their clothes don't get yucky.
3. Always wait for a grown-up to help in the kitchen.
4. Help clean up.

CONVERSIONS

Dry:
1/4 Cup = 4 tbs. = 2 oz. = 60g
1 Cup = 1/2 lb.= 8 oz. = 250g

Tip: Always level off top of measuring spoons and cups

Liquid:
1/4 Cup=2 fl. oz.=60ml
1 Cup=8 fl. oz.=250ml

The Princess And The Pea

COVER STORY

Princess Tells All!

Just between you and me, if I had been **sleeping** on a plain old **pea** I would have slept through the **night** . I was staying at the **castle** because I had gotten caught in the **rain** , and I needed a place to stay for the **night** .

While staying at the castle I learned that the **queen** was looking for a **princess** to marry her son. To find a real **princess** , she piled **twenty** **20** mattresses on top of one another, and then placed a **pea** on the bottom of the pile without letting anyone know. She believed that **one** **1** **pea** would keep a real **princess** awake. Well, I am a real **princess** , but everyone knows it's impossible for anyone to notice **one** **1** **pea** under **twenty** **20** mattresses .

However, I smelled yummy **popovers** coming from the royal **kitchen** in the middle of the **night** .

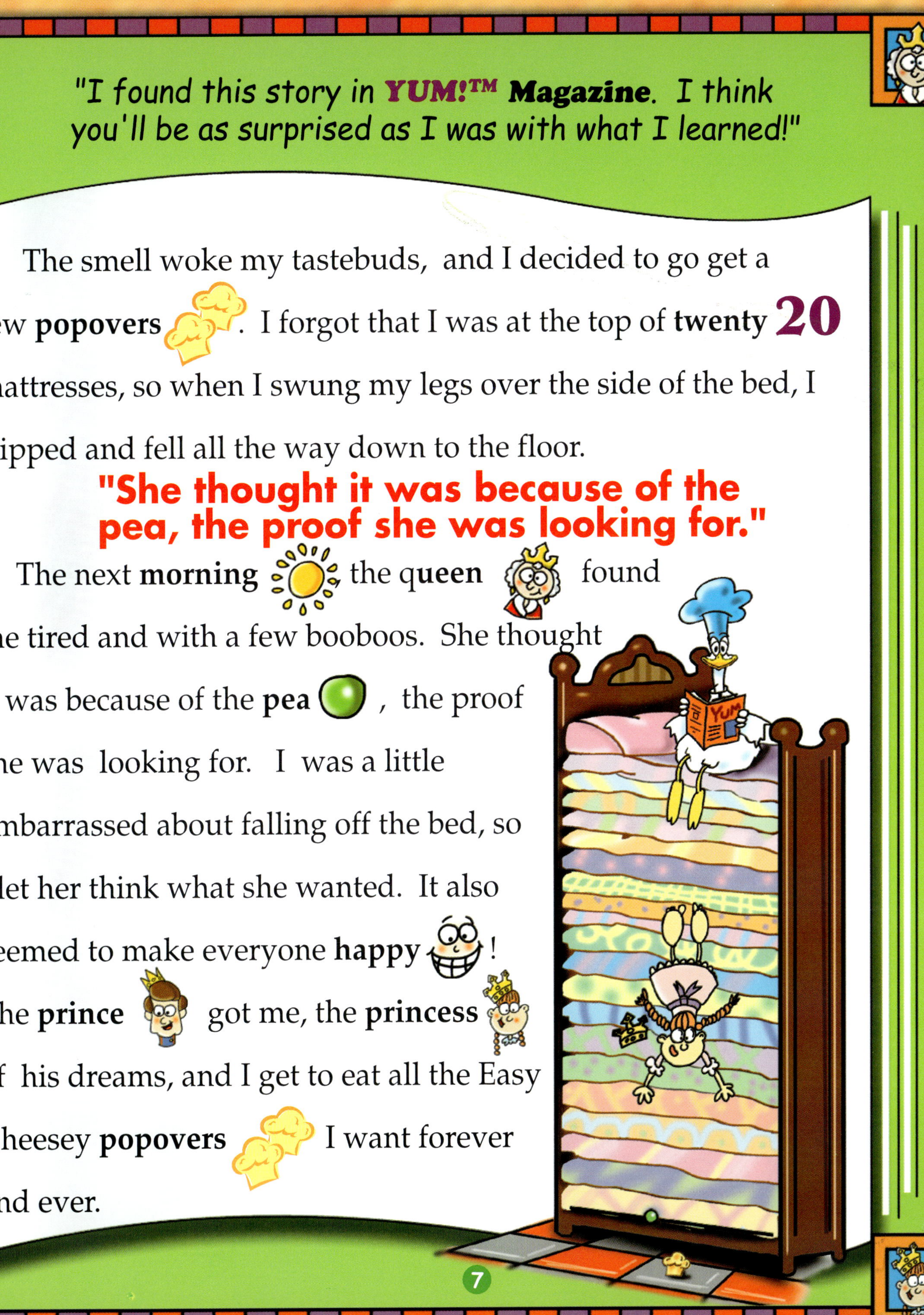

"I found this story in **YUM!™ Magazine**. I think you'll be as surprised as I was with what I learned!"

The smell woke my tastebuds, and I decided to go get a few **popovers**. I forgot that I was at the top of **twenty** **20** mattresses, so when I swung my legs over the side of the bed, I slipped and fell all the way down to the floor.

"She thought it was because of the pea, the proof she was looking for."

The next **morning** the **queen** found me tired and with a few booboos. She thought it was because of the **pea**, the proof she was looking for. I was a little embarrassed about falling off the bed, so I let her think what she wanted. It also seemed to make everyone **happy**! The **prince** got me, the **princess** of his dreams, and I get to eat all the Easy Cheesey **popovers** I want forever and ever.

Food FUNtivities

"Now let's make the yummy popovers that kept the princess awake all night!"

THE PRINCESS' EASY CHEESEY POPOVERS™

What you need:

(Makes 6)

Ingredients

1/2 tablespoon melted butter
6 frozen green peas, thawed
2 eggs
1/2 cup milk
1 tablespoon melted butter
1/4 teaspoon salt
1/2 cup shredded sharp cheddar cheese
1/2 cup flour

Goosie's Gear™

Measuring spoons
Pastry brush
6-cup muffin pan
Large bowl
Measuring cup
Fork
Large spoon
Mini ladle
Break An Egg timer
Oven mitt

How to make them:

1. Preheat the oven to 400°F.
2. Brush 1/2 tablespoon melted butter into the muffin cups with the pastry brush. Place 1 pea in the bottom of each cup for the princess.

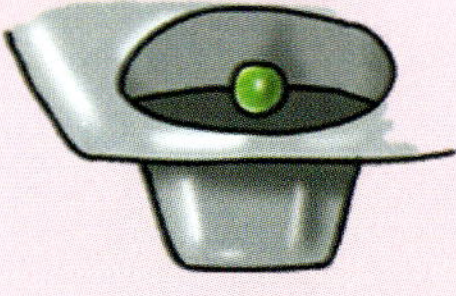

3. Place both thumbs in the middle of each egg and press until the eggs crack. Let the eggs drop into the mixing bowl and throw the shells away. (Remember to wash your hands right away.)
4. Measure the milk and add it to the eggs. Add 1 tablespoon butter and the salt. Beat it with the fork.

5. Measure the cheese and flour and add slowly to the bowl. Stir it with the large spoon just until it is mixed up. Don't mix it too much.

6. Ladle 3 spoonfuls of the batter into each muffin cup, filling them 2/3 full.
7. Place the muffin pan on the center rack of the oven. Set timer for 30 minutes. Bake the popovers until the timer rings or until they are golden brown.
8. Remove the muffin pan from the oven with the oven mitt. Prick the tops of the popover with the fork to let the steam out.

If you can taste the pea when you eat the popovers, you're a princess or a prince!

20-SECOND SUPER SMOOTHIE™

What you need: (Serves 4 to 6)

Ingredients

2 bananas, peeled
2 fresh peaches, washed, and cut into halves, or 1 small can of peaches with the juice
2 cups fresh strawberries, washed, stems removed
1 cup vanilla low-fat frozen yogurt
1 cup milk

Goosie's Gear™

Kid-friendly knife
Measuring cup
Blender

How to make it:

1. Slice each banana and peach into 4 to 6 pieces with the knife. Measure the strawberries.

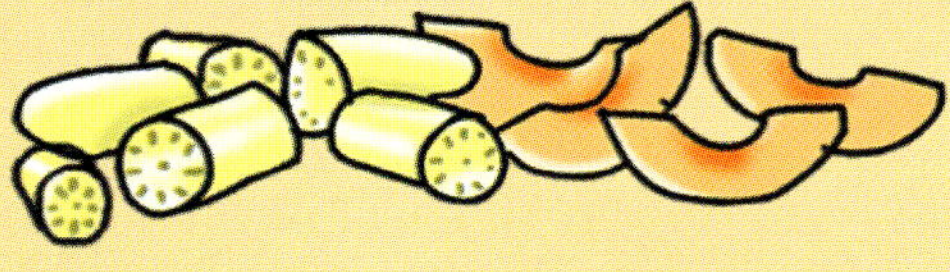

2. Place the bananas, peaches and strawberries in blender container. Measure the yogurt and milk and add it to the blender.
3. Place the top on the blender container and turn the blender on. Let the blender run while you count to 20. The smoothies are ready when they look - you guessed it! Smooth!

Counting

Goosie has spilled all the peas. He wants to pick up all the yellow peas. How many peas are there? Shelley will pick up the red ones. How many is that? If you pick up all the green ones who picked up the most peas?

(Answers on page 32)

All Peas

The Fisherman And His Wife

"I wasn't fishing for a tale when I went down to the pond with Grandpa Goosie, but that's what I caught! As I reeled in my line, I saw I had caught the Great Flounder. He told me this story. (Yes, I speak fish very well!)"

One day I was caught by a nice **fisherman** who set me free when he learned that I was really an enchanted **prince**. The problem was the **fisherman's** **wife**. She thought I, the **Great Flounder** , owed them for her husband's kindness, and so she told her husband to ask me to grant them a wish for a new **house**, which I gave them. But, the **fisherman's** **wife** wanted more!

Next, she wanted a **castle**, and then she wished to be **queen**. Finally, she wished to control **day** and **night**! Imagine! Well, **I** had enough of the **wife's** wishes, and I took away everything I had given them. I returned the **fisherman** and his **wife** to their humble little **shack**, which by the way, made the **fisherman** very **happy**.

"So, remember **Goosie**, the **Great Flounder** said, "It's OK to wish for stuff, but don't get too greedy or you may end up with **zero** 0!"

Food FUNtivities

"It's time to go fish and create some fishy food fun!"

GONE FISHIN' RODS™

(Makes 2 Rods)

What you need:

Ingredients

2 red string candy
2 pretzel rods or long breadsticks
Small package of gummie worms
1/2 package of goldfish crackers
Peanut butter or cream cheese

Goosie's Gear™

Small plastic bowl
Spreading knife

How to make them:

1. Tie the candy string to 1 end of the pretzel rod or breadstick, looping it once like you tie your shoe (I asked Mother Goosie to help me, and you can ask your mommy to help you too!)

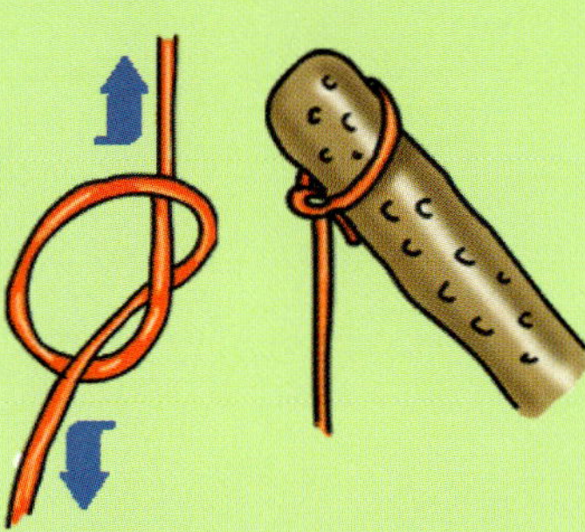

2. Tie a gummie worm to the other end of the candy string just like you tied it to the pretzel rod.

3. Pour the goldfish crackers into a small plastic bowl.

4. Place a dab of peanut butter or cream cheese on the gummie worm with the spreading knife.

5. Now go fish! Use your fishing rod to catch the goldfish and reel them in. If you eat your bait along with the fish you catch just add more peanut butter or cream cheese and gummie worms. You can even eat the rod and line when you finish fishing!

GREAT FLOUNDER SANDWICHES™

(Makes 2 Great Flounders)

What you need:

Ingredients

1 soft hoagie roll, sliced into halves the long way
4 tablespoons peanut butter
16 mandarin orange slices
1/2 cup plain or flavored O-shaped cereal
2 miniature marshmallows
2 mini M&M's
6 candy corn pieces

Goosie's Gear™

Tray
Measuring spoon
Kid-friendly knife
Measuring cup

How to make them:

1. Place the hoagie halves on a tray with the smooth sides facing up. Make the flounders' tails by cutting out a small triangle at one end of each hoagie half with the knife.

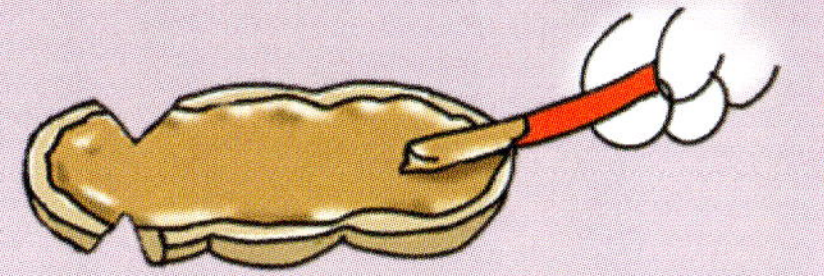

2. Spread half the peanut butter over each hoagie half.

3. Arrange 4 of the orange slices at each tail for the tail fins.

4. Measure cereal and cover each flounder with half the cereal for the scales.

5. Place one miniature marshmallow at each head end for the eye and place a miniature M&M in the middle of each marshmallow.

6. Arrange 2 of the orange slices for each top fin, 1 orange slice for each side fin and 1 slice for each mouth.

7. Arrange 3 candy corn pieces next to each top fin for a crown. Now he's an enchanted prince!

Munch on this great sandwich with a great big glass of milk!

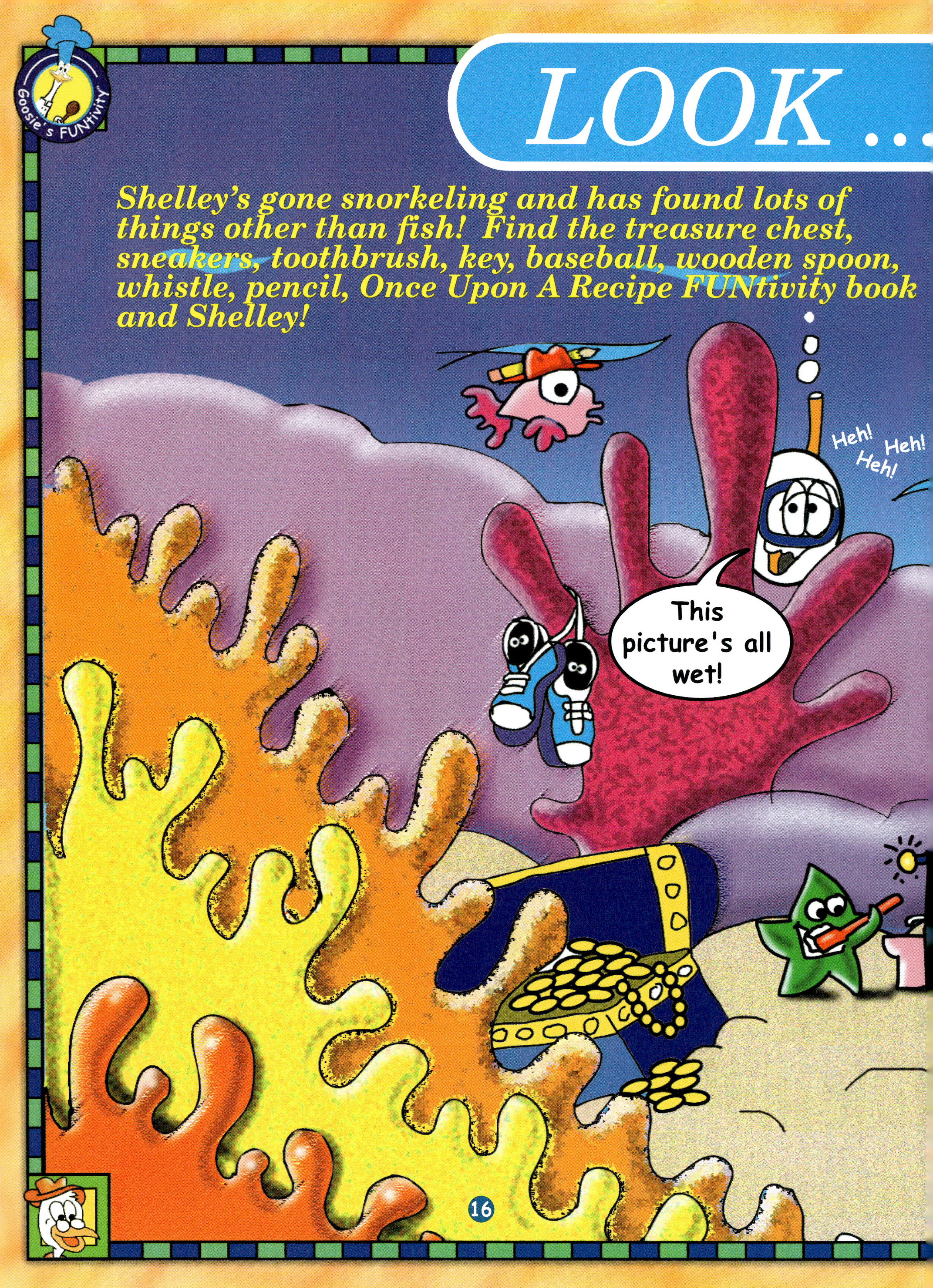
Goosie's FUNtivity
LOOK ...
Shelley's gone snorkeling and has found lots of things other than fish! Find the treasure chest, sneakers, toothbrush, key, baseball, wooden spoon, whistle, pencil, Once Upon A Recipe FUNtivity book and Shelley!
Heh! Heh! Heh!
This picture's all wet!

& FIND

(Answers on page 32)

The Three Little Pigs

"The Three Little Pigs brought me this letter from The Big Bad Wolf. I'd like to share it with you."

Dear **Goosie**,

Remember how I huffed and puffed and blew down the little **pigs'** **houses**? Well, I wasn't huffing and puffing, I was aaah-chooing and coughing around the **clock**. I had a very bad cold and needed a **box of tissues** 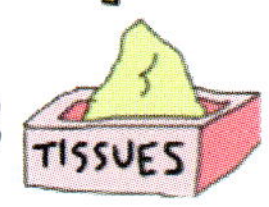

for my *Big Bad* ***Nose***  !

Well, **pigs**  have pretty big **noses** 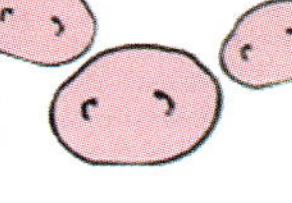 too, so I figured they'd have a **box of tissues** 

. But, when I got to the first **pig's**  **house**  to ask for some, I started aaah-chooing and accidentally blew down his **house** of **straw** .

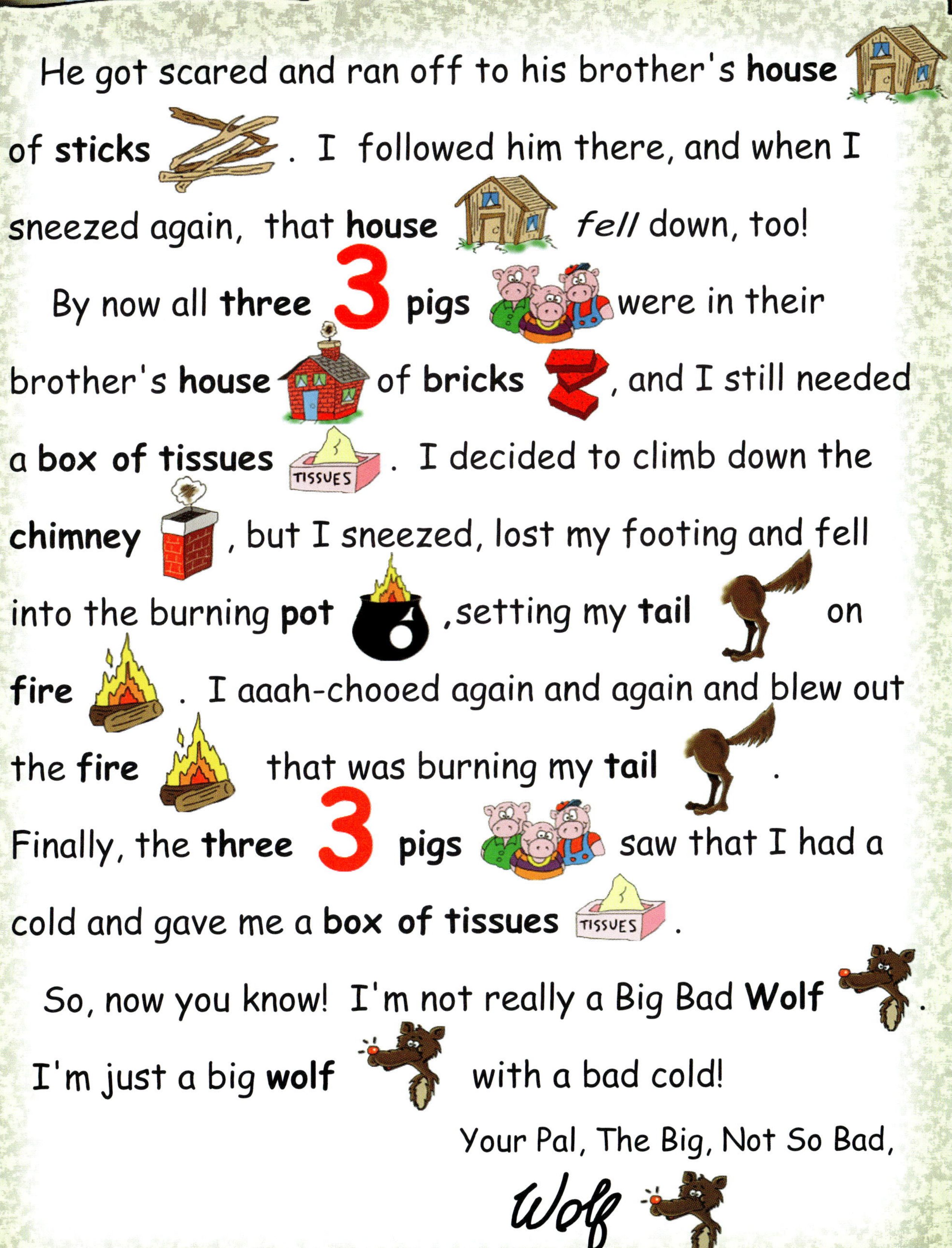

He got scared and ran off to his brother's **house** of **sticks**. I followed him there, and when I sneezed again, that **house** *fell* down, too!

By now all **three** 3 **pigs** were in their brother's **house** of **bricks**, and I still needed a **box of tissues**. I decided to climb down the **chimney**, but I sneezed, lost my footing and fell into the burning **pot**, setting my **tail** on **fire**. I aaah-chooed again and again and blew out the **fire** that was burning my **tail**. Finally, the **three** 3 **pigs** saw that I had a cold and gave me a **box of tissues**.

So, now you know! I'm not really a Big Bad **Wolf**. I'm just a big **wolf** with a bad cold!

Your Pal, The Big, Not So Bad,

Wolf

"The three little pigs love to make pig-tures of themselves, so I created these pizzas. They're yummy and pig-ture perfect!"

PIG-FACED PIZZAS™

What you need:

(Makes 4)

Ingredients

Sauce*

1 small can tomato paste
1/8 teaspoon garlic powder
1/2 teaspoon onion powder
1/4 teaspoon dried oregano
1/4 teaspoon dried basil
1/4 teaspoon salt
1/4 teaspoon pepper
1 tablespoon olive oil

2 large English muffins, split in half

3/4 cup shredded mozzarella cheese

Goosie's Gear™

Medium bowl
Measuring spoons
Wooden spoon
Baking sheet
Mini ladle
Measuring cup
Turner
Oven mitt

Break An Egg™ timer

* You can also use 1/4 cup ready-made sauce

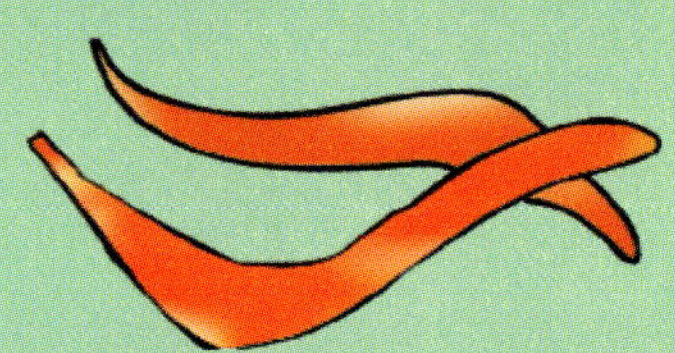

Face decorations:

Eyes: 8 thin carrot slices, small cooked green peas or black olive slices

Nose: 4 mushroom slices

Mouth: 4 red bell pepper strips

Ears: 8 cherry tomato halves or turkey pepperoni slices

How to make them:

1. Preheat oven to 375°F.

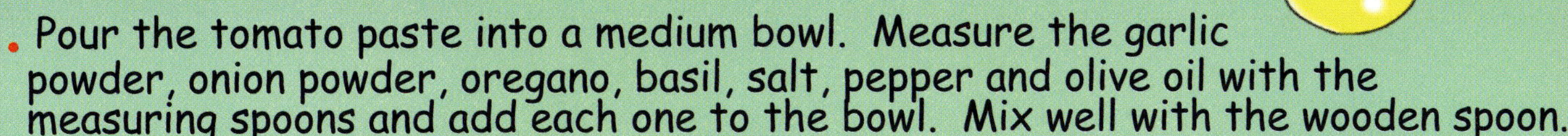

2. Pour the tomato paste into a medium bowl. Measure the garlic powder, onion powder, oregano, basil, salt, pepper and olive oil with the measuring spoons and add each one to the bowl. Mix well with the wooden spoon.

3. Place the muffins on the baking sheet and use the ladle to spoon the sauce onto the muffins. Spread the sauce to the edges with the wooden spoon.

4. Measure the mozzarella cheese and sprinkle it over the muffins to cover them completely.

5. Decorate the faces!

6. Set the timer for 10 minutes. Place the baking sheet on the center oven rack. Bake the muffins until the timer rings or until the cheese is melted. Use the oven mitt to take the baking sheet out of the oven. Remove the pizzas with the turner.

LET'S PIG OUT!

THE THREE LITTLE PIGS BERRY PINK LEMONADE™

(Makes 4 cups)

What you need:

Ingredients

6 lemons, cut into halves
1/4 cup sugar
3 cups water
1 cup cranberry juice
Ice

Goosie's Gear™

Juicer
Wooden spoon
Pitcher
Measuring spoons
Measuring cup
Glasses

How to make it:

1. Press the lemon halves as hard as you can over a juicer to remove the juice or squeeze the juice into a small bowl. Remove the seeds with the wooden spoon and pour the juice into the pitcher.

2. Use the measuring spoons to measure the sugar and add it to the lemon juice. Stir it until it dissolves.

3. Use the measuring cup to measure the water and cranberry juice and pour it into the pitcher. Stir it to mix it well.

4. Pour the lemonade over the ice in the glasses.

What's

Find 10 things that are different between these two pictures!

Different?

(Answers on page 32)

Little Red Riding Hood

"As I was walking through the forest the other day with Grandma Goosie, I ran into Little Red Riding Hood who was in a great rush carrying a basket of biscuits for her new friend, the wolf. When I asked her how the wolf had become her new friend she told me to follow her and she'd explain."

I'm sure you've heard of how I stopped to talk to the **wolf**. Well, I shouldn't have done that, but thanks to me, the **wolf** is now a better-to-meet person. It all happened after the **wolf** tricked me into telling him that I was going to my **Grandma's** **house,** even though my **mommy** told me to *never* to talk to strangers.

When the **wolf** arrived at **Grandma's**, he found my sweet **Grandma** asleep upstairs and gobbled her down in a flash. After all, he told me later, he is a **wolf** and it was **lunchtime**!

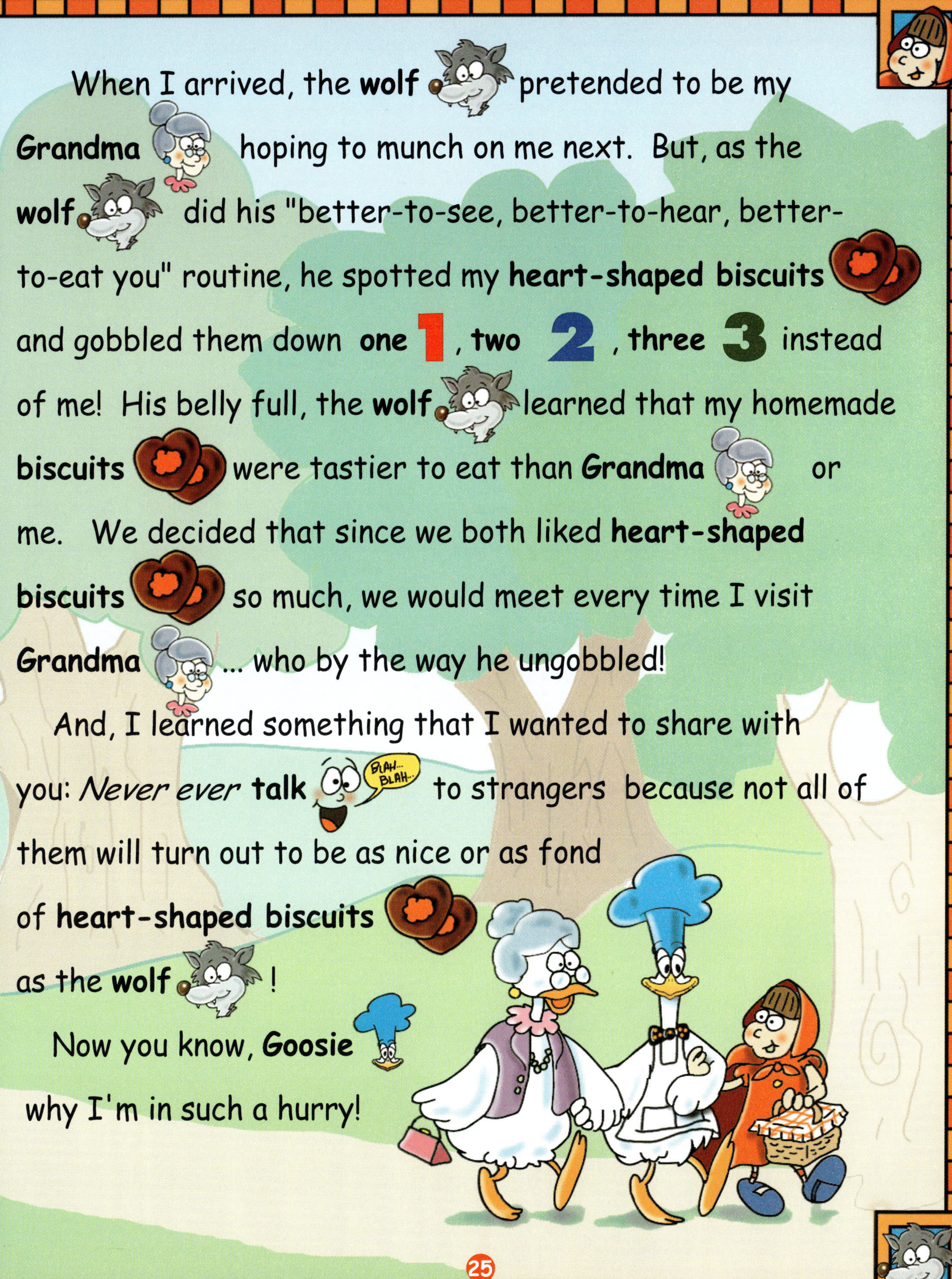

When I arrived, the **wolf** pretended to be my **Grandma** hoping to munch on me next. But, as the **wolf** did his "better-to-see, better-to-hear, better-to-eat you" routine, he spotted my **heart-shaped biscuits** and gobbled them down **one** 1, **two** 2, **three** 3 instead of me! His belly full, the **wolf** learned that my homemade **biscuits** were tastier to eat than **Grandma** or me. We decided that since we both liked **heart-shaped biscuits** so much, we would meet every time I visit **Grandma** ... who by the way he ungobbled!

And, I learned something that I wanted to share with you: *Never ever* **talk** to strangers because not all of them will turn out to be as nice or as fond of **heart-shaped biscuits** as the **wolf** !

Now you know, **Goosie** why I'm in such a hurry!

Food FUNtivities

"These biscuits are even "better to eat" when you serve them with the wolf's Better-To Drink Punch!"

LITTLE RED'S GOOEY HEART-SHAPED BISCUITS™

(Makes 8)

What you need:

Ingredients

2 1/4 cups prepared biscuit mix
2/3 cup milk
1 1/2 tablespoons melted butter
Flour
Strawberry preserves

Goosie's Gear™

Measuring cup
Large bowl
Wooden spoon
Rolling pin
Heart-shaped cookie cutter
Baking sheet
Measuring spoon
Oven mitt
Break An Egg™ timer
Turner

How to make them:

1. Preheat oven to 450°F. Measure the biscuit mix, milk and butter and combine them in a large bowl. Mix them with the wooden spoon until they form a dough.

2. Dump the dough onto a counter sprinkled with flour. Fold and push the dough down 10 times.

3. Roll the dough with the rolling pin until it is about as thick as your thumb.

4. Cut out 8 biscuits with the heart-shaped cookie cutter. Pick up the biscuits gently and place them on the baking sheet.

5. Press down in the middle of each biscuit to make a dent. Spoon 1/2 teaspoon of the preserves into each dent.

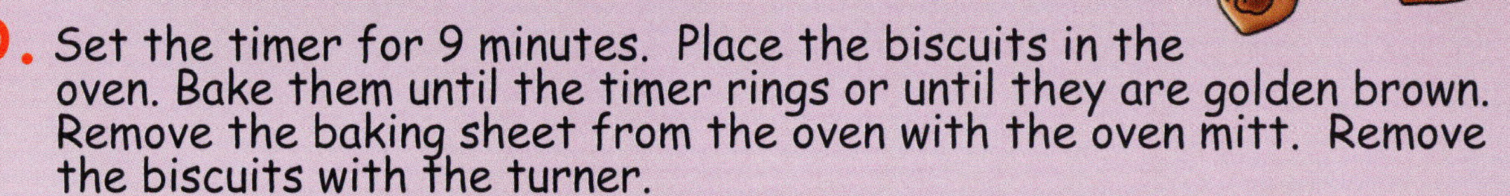

6. Set the timer for 9 minutes. Place the biscuits in the oven. Bake them until the timer rings or until they are golden brown. Remove the baking sheet from the oven with the oven mitt. Remove the biscuits with the turner.

Be sure to let the biscuits cool a little before eating them so they aren't too hot!

BETTER-TO-DRINK™ ORANGE PUNCH

(Makes 4 cups)

What you need:

Ingredients

Ice Cubes:
8 fresh strawberries, cut into halves
1 cup cranberry juice

Punch:
8 or 9 large oranges, cut into halves
1 cup cranberry juice
1 cup ginger ale

Goosie's Gear™

Kid-friendly knife
Ice cube tray
Measuring cup
Juicer
Pitcher
Wooden spoon
Glasses

How to make it:

How you make the ice cubes:

1. Place 1 strawberry half into each compartment of the ice cube tray.
2. Measure the cranberry juice and pour it into the ice cube tray.
3. Place the tray in the freezer for 2 hours or until the juice freezes.

How you make the punch:

1. Press the halves of 8 oranges as hard as you can to remove the juice. Measure the orange juice, and if it does not measure 2 cups, squeeze the other orange. Pour the juice into the pitcher.

2. Measure the cranberry juice and ginger ale and add it to the pitcher. Stir it with the wooden spoon.

3. Pour the punch into the glasses. Twist the ice cube trays to remove the ice cubes and place the cubes in the glasses.
4. Before you drink the punch, say "Break An Egg!" Remember that means good luck and good health in Goose!

Goosie's FUNtivity
A-Maze-ing
SLOW!!
Turtle
Crossing

Journey

Help Little Red Riding Hood get to Grandma's house. Find 10 yummy and healthy kinds of foods along the way.

(Answers on page 32)

Goosie's FUNtivity
Alphabet.
Find the things in Goosie's kitchen that begin with each letter of the alphabet.
Today's forcast... scattered juice all day!
Heh! Heh! Heh!
B

...Search

Here's one to get you started. "A" is for Apple!

(Answers on page 32)

FUNtivity ANSWERS

Yellow peas=20 Red peas=30 Green peas=40

1. PENCIL 2. SHELLEY 3. SNEAKERS 4. TOOTHBRUSH 5. TREASURE CHEST 6. WHISTLE 7. BASEBALL 8. WOODEN SPOON 9 . KEY 10. ONCE UPON A RECIPE BOOK

1. Blue curtains 2. Cloud missing 3. Wolf missing 4. Orange tree leaves 5. One hot dog 6. Red overalls 7. Blue swing 8. Door Open 9 . One butterfly missing 10. Pig is facing different way

1. Pasta 2. Apples 3. Cheese 4. Drumstick 5. Banana 6. Oranges 7. Carrots 8. Eggs 9 . Milk 10. Bread and Butter

A-Apple
B-Butter
C-Cupcake
D-Donuts
E-Eggs
F-Fisherman
G-Goosie
H-Hat
I-Ice Cream
J-Jelly Beans
K-Kite
L-Little Red Riding Hood
M-Mouse
N-Napkin
O-Oven
P-Princess
Q-Queen
R-Rolling Pin
S-Shelley
T-Tea Kettle
U-Umbrella
V-Violin
W-Wolf
X-Xray
Y-Yarn
Z-Zebra